For my father, Paul Sultan, for filling my
childhood with outdoor adventures and
a love of nature. May the song of the
White-throated Sparrow always be the most
beautiful sound you've ever heard—J. W.

For my family, and the good people of the
Chicago Field Museum's Bird Division—D. S.

BEACH LANE BOOKS
An imprint of Simon & Schuster Children's Publishing Division
1230 Avenue of the Americas, New York, New York 10020
Text copyright © 2020 by Jennifer Ward
Illustrations copyright © 2020 by Diana Sudyka
All rights reserved, including the right of reproduction in whole or in part in any form.
BEACH LANE BOOKS is a trademark of Simon & Schuster, Inc.
For information about special discounts for bulk purchases, please contact Simon & Schuster Special Sales
at 1-866-506-1949 or business@simonandschuster.com.
The Simon & Schuster Speakers Bureau can bring authors to your live event. For more information or to book an event,
contact the Simon & Schuster Speakers Bureau at 1-866-248-3049 or visit our website at www.simonspeakers.com.
Book design by Lauren Rille
The text for this book was set in New Century Schoolbook.
The illustrations for this book were rendered in watercolor gouache on paper, and finished digitally.
Manufactured in China
0521 SCP
10 9 8 7 6 5 4 3 2
Library of Congress Cataloging-in-Publication Data
Names: Ward, Jennifer, 1963– author. | Sudyka, Diana, illustrator.
Title: How to find a bird / Jennifer Ward ; illustrated by Diana Sudyka.
Description: First edition. | New York : Beach Lane Books, [2020] | Summary: A nonfiction guide to finding
and observing birds for young bird-watchers.—Provided by publisher.
Identifiers: LCCN 2019027861 (print) | ISBN 9781481467056 (hardcover) | ISBN 9781481467063 (eBook)
Subjects: LCSH: Bird-watching—Juvenile literature.
Classification: LCC QL677.5.W3345 2020 (print) | DDC 598.072/34—dc23
LC record available at https://lccn.loc.gov/2019027861

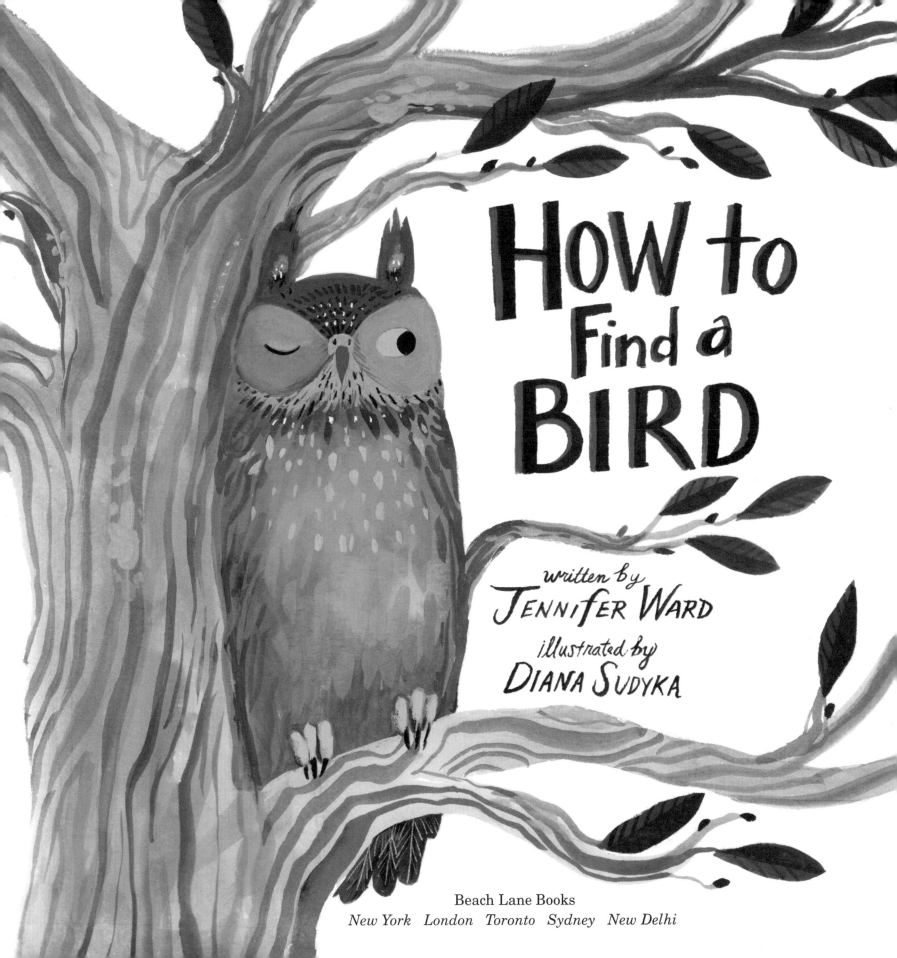

HOW to Find a BIRD

written by
JENNIFER WARD

illustrated by
DIANA SUDYKA

Beach Lane Books
New York   London   Toronto   Sydney   New Delhi

There are a lot of ways to find a bird.

Pigeon or Rock Dove

House Sparrow

That's the wonderful thing about birds.

To find a bird,
first you'll want to blend in.

American Bittern

Great Blue Heron

Mallard

And move slowly.

California Quail

Quiet is good too.
So quiet you can hear
your heartbeat.

Shhhhhhh

Tundra Swan

Barn Swallow

Northern Cardinal

American Robin

Eastern Bluebird

Don't just look up to find a bird.

Look down, low to the ground
where some birds forage,
seeking things hiding in the earth.

White-throated Sparrow

Northern Flicker

Look down
where some birds sneak snacks.

Look down
where some birds splash.

Roseatte Spoonbill

Anhinga

Ring-billed Gull

Least Sandpiper

If you take a walk, watch your step.
Some birds nest on the ground.

Burrowing
Owl

Steller's Jay

So don't just look up
to find a bird.

Sometimes you can find a bird
by looking straight ahead.
You will have to have a sharp eye.

Sharp as an eagle's eye.

Birds are the cleverest
blenders of all.

Eastern Whip-poor-will

Long-eared Owl

Brown Creeper

At first you may not see them.
But if you wait, if you are still,
and if you are quiet,
you'll see.

You are just as clever as a bird.

Of course you can always
look up to find a bird too!

Canada Goose

Purple Martin

Rufous
Hummingbird

Golden-crowned
Kinglet

Western Tanager

American Kestrel

Monk Parakeet

Scissor-tailed Flycatcher

Baltimore Oriole

Goldfinch

Tree Swallow

You can look up high in the sky,
where birds fly.

Sometimes when you look up,
you'll find birds simply sitting.

European Starling

Red-tailed
Hawk

If you could perch
high in the sky . . .

a murmuration

of Starlings

what might *you* see?

If you want to find a bird, don't be tricked.
Some birds are stealthy.

Peregrine Falcon

There it is!

Wait a minute. Where'd it go?

Was that even a bird?

Sometimes you don't
need to find a bird.

Mourning Dove

It will find you.

Hello, bluebird!

Eastern Bluebird

HOME SWEET HOME

Some birds will announce their presence when they are near.

Or announce *your* presence
when they see you.

JAY!

JAY!

JAY!

JAY!

JAY!

Hello, jay!

Blue Jay

And if you feed them,
they will come.

Downy Woodpecker

Northern Cardinal (male)

Northern Cardinal (female)

Black-capped Chickadee

White-breasted Nuthatch

Common Grackle

American Robin

Dark-eyed Junco

Mourning Dove

Red-bellied Woodpecker

Brown Creeper

Ruby-throated Hummingbird

Then all you need is a window to find a bird.

Some birds can't be found at all,
unless you read about them.

Dodo

Passenger Pigeon

Ivory-billed Woodpecker

Carolina Parakeet

Dusky Seaside Sparrow

These birds are extinct,
which means they no longer exist.

But the best way to find a bird,
if you want to find one,
is to close your eyes.

Did you hear that?

Did you hear that bird?

That's the wonderful thing about birds.

Whooping Crane

We can all be bird watchers!

Bird-watching is as simple as opening our ears and eyes to the sights and sounds around us. From urban spaces to wild places, even through a window—birds can be found everywhere! And the great thing is, bird-watching doesn't require a lot of work—just the practice of being aware of their presence. It can be done for as short or as long a time as you want, during any time of day, during any season. Are you ready to find a bird?

Here are some ways to get started:

Tools and Tips

A simple set of binoculars can be helpful to watch birds, but they're not necessary. A *lot* can be seen with the naked eye, such as a bird's general size, shape, color pattern, and behavior. As you spot birds, it's fun to learn to identify them. It's like a game *and* a challenge! Try these strategies:

Note details. All birds have feathers, but not all birds behave the same way or live in the same places. Most eat bugs, but some, like the American Goldfinch, eat only seeds, while others, such as birds of prey, hunt for small animals to eat. Some spend much of their time high in treetops, while others feed and even nest on or near the ground. Noting details like these helps us learn about each species:

- Location: Where was the bird seen or heard? On the ground? In a tree? Near water? At a bird feeder? Alone? In a flock?

- Size: Was it tiny, like a hummingbird? Small, like a finch? Medium, like a mockingbird? Large, like a hawk or heron?

- Behavior: How did the bird act? Did it hop on the ground? Scale a tree? Perch and sing? Wade along a shoreline? Did it make any interesting movements, such as bobbing its tail up and down?

- Description: Was its tail long or short? Did the tail point upward, or downward? What shape was its beak?

Use a field guide to birds in your area to help learn what species are in your region year-round, for nesting season, or just passing through during migration.

Check out *Merlin Bird ID*, a free app for all ages designed by the Cornell Lab of Ornithology. It uses five easy questions, starting with: *What size was the bird?* and *What were the main colors?* You can even upload a photo of the bird for its visual-recognition component.

Northern Cardinal

Look for field marks—the distinctive stripes, colors, spots, or patterns that are found on birds. Some field marks include:

- Beak color: the color of the upper beak and lower beak
- Eyebrow stripe: a line over the eye
- Eyeline: a line through the eye

- Eye-ring: a ring of color around the eye
- Throat patch: a patch of color, such as white, on the throat
- Wingbars: stripes on the wing

Create a Life List
Keep a list of the different bird species you see, noting where and when each was observed:
Date:
Location:
Time:
Bird:
You'll be amazed to see your list grow over time!

Wild Turkey   Downy Woodpecker

Become a Citizen Scientist
Researchers, conservation biologists, and others who study birds will appreciate your observations, which provide a bigger picture of the health and status of bird populations. Opportunities for bird-related citizen science projects include bird counts, such as:

Audubon Christmas Bird Count (audubon.org /conservation/science/christmas-bird-count): Sign-up begins in November each year, with counting taking place from December 14 to January 5.

Global Big Day (ebird.org/globalbigday): For one twenty-four-hour period each year in early May, people all over the world are encouraged to count birds they see and then share their findings.

The Great Backyard Bird Count (gbbc .birdcount.org): Count the birds you see each year in February during President's Day weekend.

Journey North (journeynorth.org): Help track migration patterns. Report your first-of-the-season sightings of many types of birds, such as American Robins, Bald Eagles, Barn Swallows, Common Loons, Red-winged Blackbirds, Whooping Cranes, hummingbirds, orioles, and songbirds.

Visit JenniferWardBooks.com for a list of books about birds and birdwatching.

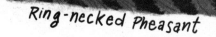
Ring-necked Pheasant